Flowing In Faith

Visionary:

Bernadette M. Brawner

Written and Created by Visionary, Author Bernadette M. Brawner

BernadetteMBrawner@gmail.com | 202-838-7363

Forward by Denise Victoria McAllister

Cover Designed by Camden Lane Creative Agency

www.camdenlanecreative.com

Publishing Services provided by Lynda D. Mallory

www.lyndadmallory.com

Biblical Reference unless otherwise noted, scripture references were taken from the King James, New King James Version, New Living Translation of the Holy Bible.

ISBN: 978-0-578-82434-5

Printed in the United States of America

DEDICATION

This book is dedicated to YOU!

Dear brothers and sisters, when troubles of any kind come your way, consider it an opportunity for great joy. For you know that when your faith is tested, your endurance has a chance to grow. ~ James 1:2-3 NLT

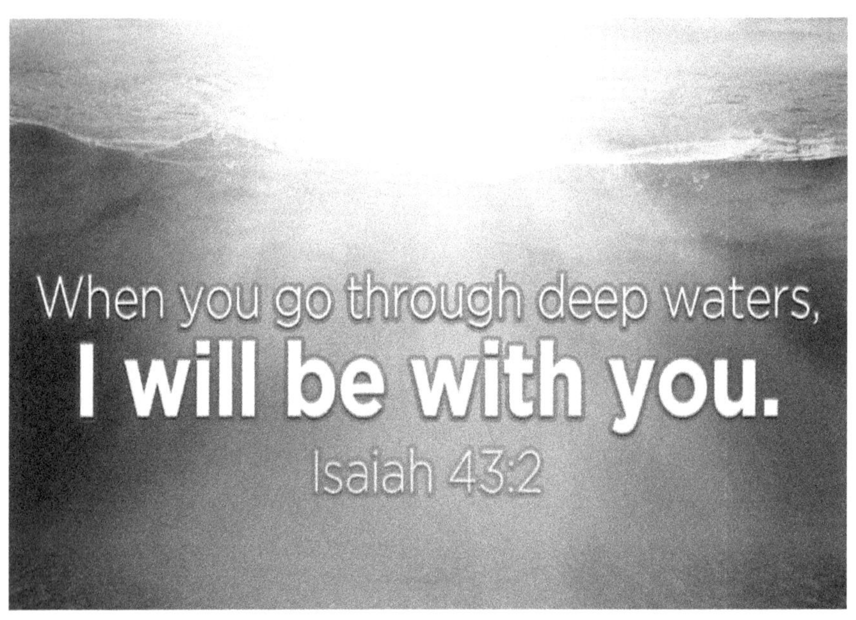
When you go through deep waters,
I will be with you.
Isaiah 43:2

CONTENTS

FOREWARD i
Dr. Denise Victoria McAllister i

INTRODUCTION vi
By Bernadette M. Brawner vi

FAITH LIKE A MARRIAGE VOW 4
By Michelle Boulden-Hammond 4

RENEWING IN FAITH 14
By Ina Smith 14

FAITH PHENOMENON 27
By Dr. Denise Victoria McAllister 27

GOD'S PRESENCE IN THE MIDST OF THE UNTHINKABLE. 44
By Debra Thornton 44

MAKING OF A DIAMOND THROUGH FAITH 55
By Dr. Astril Webb 55

FAITH ALWAYS BRINGS VICTORY 67
By Bernadette M Brawner 67

FAITH IN ACTION 81
Growing Deeper In Faith 81
Practical Steps To Walking In Faith 81

FAITH IN ACTION 84
Growing Deeper In Faith 84
Use These Pages To Capture Your Thoughts And Write Your Story/Testimony 84

FOREWARD

Dr. Denise Victoria McAllister

What an honor and privilege to be asked to write the Forward for Flowing In Faith, composed by Bernadette Brawner.

When Bernadette Brawner asked me to write the Forward for her book on Flowing N Faith©. I don't think I hesitated for one minute to say Yes! Bernadette is one of the most loving and caring individuals I have met. She has been placed by God in a category of benevolence wherein her heart reaches out to assist in the most unusual situations and circumstances. For her to write a book on Faith is no surprise to me. Bernadette is not only a testament of how much she loves God, and people; it is also a testament of her divine purpose in life.

I met Bernadette Brawner back in 2016 having been invited as a Guest Speaker for S.H.E.E.'s Empowerment Summit. We talked for the first time over the telephone and our spirits connected immediately, realizing this was a God ordained relationship. It is not the length of time we have known an individual that matters. It is the depth of that relationship and the results of the fruit produced in the relationship that matters.

I watched how Bernadette put her heart and soul in this event never giving up, no matter how the attacks came and presented themselves. S.H.E.E.'s Empowerment Summit was outstanding and victorious to say the least. The accompanied speakers were on point in sharing what God had done in their lives. The Speakers shared where they came from and where they were today by the Glory of God. Which if we look in retrospect Flowing In Faith is the manifestation of the same, *Sharing and Caring.*

Bernadette Brawner's educational and work experience is par-excellent. When I first read her Curriculum Vitae, I was floored to know this woman who acquired and achieved so much in her life in education and in the Federal Government was such a humbled, submitted Woman of Faith.

The Bible declares, when we humble ourselves, we shall be exalted. I Peter 5:6 Exalting is exactly what the Lord is truly doing through this book and the things that will follow its publication.

Flowing In Faith will illuminate, excite, bring tears to your eyes, and ignite a fire in you towards Faith that you may have never ever experienced. Faith is REAL, ALIVE and WELL. Faith does not die during adverse situations. Faith is in fact in these adverse situations most relevant.

Bernadette's testimonies of Faith will set you on a path of divine appointment. The other authors in Flowing In Faith have been handpicked by Bernadette, after much prayer and direction by Holy Spirit. I have no doubt their stories will become *Best Sellers* along with this book reaching heights they could have never imagined. I decree doors of opportunity will open for each writer who has joined in this phenomenal, purposed vision. As well as those who will support this endeavor. Bernadette Brawner is good ground. Selah

Flowing In Faith are stories from individuals who have gone through tremendous test and trials. Having witnessed God's miraculous provision, peace, healing, and deliverance without equivocation. These writers are sharing from their hearts what they know for sure. They have done the work and now have the ability as well as the opportunity to go to another level of life by letting their experiences go and grow to help others through their walk-in life.

This book should be in everyone's library. In High Schools, and Collegiate settings, whether Christian or not - the words in Flowing In Faith demonstrate the significant of the subject matter in everyone's life.

Without Faith We Cannot Please God. Hebrews 11:6 The Bible does not say without Love We Cannot Please God – the Word of God clearly declares Without Faith We Cannot Please God. Clarifying it *takes Faith to Love.* That which is not Faith is sin. Romans 14:23b

Whether we are in testing times or times of bliss - when it seems like everything in our lives is going well – Faith is still required and necessary. It is imperative that we Walk by Faith, Live by Faith and Speak Faith words over our daily lives.

Flowing In Faith shares these Principles:

1. What Faith is*
2. Knowing How to Activate Faith*
3. The Results of Walking by Faith*
4. The Power and Ability of Sharing Faith with Others*
5. We Overcome by Faith and the words of our Testimony*

As mentioned earlier, Bernadette is a Woman of Faith. A strong woman and a dedicated mother to her daughter, Makeala. I have personally witnessed God's faithfulness in her life. She is more than qualified to release FLOWING IN FAITH. As you read throughout the pages of this book you shall receive. Faith is not selfish or limited to any race, color, gender, or creed. Faith is available to those who have received – God has given to every man and woman the measure of Faith. Romans 12:3

Jesus said I came unto my own and my own received me not, but as many as receive me to them I give the power to become the sons and daughters of God. John 1:11-12 As sons and daughters of God we are given certain rights and privileges that are not available to others.

It is written I believed; therefore, I have spoken. Since we have that same spirit of Faith, we also believe and therefore speak. 2 Corinthians 4:13

Flowing In Faith is not a Fairy Tale book nor a book of Fiction. These are real stories from real people who have been anointed by God for this time and beyond. Not only have these Faith miraculous events happened for the writers in this book - but similar events can also and will happen for you, when you believe and exercise the principles of Faith. Know that Faith without Works is Dead. James 2:20 Believe the words written in this book and you will begin to start FLOWING IN FAITH.

INTRODUCTION

By Bernadette M. Brawner

Author/Motivational Speaker/Professional and Financial Coach

This project was birthed out of my desire to bring hope to the hopeless. We are living in perilous times, but God is still blessing His people. I believe that it is our, (Christians), responsibility to share the goodness of God and how He has kept us. The world needs to know that our God is faithful and is worth keeping.

My vision is for each co-author to share their story of how their faith sustain them during a time of distress, health crisis, death of love one, job loss, marriage, divorce, singleness, waiting season, or a fiery test in any area of your life. These testimonies will encourage and bring healing to a society that is in desperate need of knowing the love of Christ or need reconciliation with Christ. We must share practical steps of faith that allowed us to keep God centered in our lives and not give up during our crisis. God will see us through our storm. We are living proof of this and the world needs to read/hear about it. **Pray, Trust, Believe, and be Obedient to the living word of Jesus Christ. God is JUST and FAITHFUL!**

Flowing In Faith

Vignettes

FAITH LIKE A MARRIAGE VOW

By Michelle Boulden-Hammond

FAITH LIKE A MARRIAGE VOW

By Michelle Boulden-Hammond

First, I would like to take the opportunity for you the reader to understand that this is not by chance that you have come across this book. My prayer is that you will gain a deeper level of faith and the reminder that you are more than a conqueror. I will give you a question to ponder: Have you considered the differences between faith and a vow? You are probably saying to yourself what kind of question is that to ask. Please hear me that this will come together soon by the completion of this chapter. Second, let me give you some clarity between the word's faith and vow. For instance, the word faith is defined as having trust or confidence in someone or something. It is recorded that the word faith appears 336 times in the King James Version Bible. The word vow means a committed response such as an oath dedicated to someone or something a completely solemn promise. Would you say that this is something just like a marriage? In other words, you must have faith, which trusts the vow because of the dedication to the purposeful outcome.

Let me share a bit of my journey and how my faith is now to the point that I am committed to follow no matter what I see and believing in the unseen. The bible clearly speaks in Hebrews 11:1 of faith being a substance or assurance of things hoped for but have not yet been received.

Thirty years ago, I can tell you about a woman who was a single mother living in her car with her son. Each night this family slept in the car at the county's health department during the night. The woman I am describing is me. I would wake up, take a bath, and get dressed at my aunt's house because my son would go there for daycare while I attended work. You as the reader probably are asking yourself why wouldn't she just stay with her family? Well, my family did not know because of my pride of not asking for help. I could not let my family see that my boyfriend had thrown me out. It was hard to make ends meet with working a part-time job as cafeteria lunch lady.

I would pray often-asking God to send me some help to get me out this situation and find sustainability of housing and a decent job. One day it was time for recertification of medical assistance for my son and I was called into the department of social services for a meeting for the completion of my paperwork. I met with the social worker and she asked me was there anything else that I needed. I told her no I did not. She replied are you sure, because I had a certain look on my face that I did. I gathered my belongings, left the building as I entered my car, and turned on the radio an old gospel hymn was on "Just a Little Talk with Jesus."

For some reason I will tell you I usually would have on V103 and until this day, I do not recall changing the station to gospel music. After hearing this song play, it reminded me of the conversation that I had with the social worker and how she distinctively asked, was there anything else I needed. I pondered and I pondered, but then I realized God clearly had set me up. I had been asking God to remove me from a situation but clearly was going to pass it up. So, I called into the office crying on the line and guess who answered the hotline the same caseworker. She immediately found me housing and place for me and my son to live with rental assistance for 6 months.

Now let me tell you that in this testimony I am telling you that I had to put in the work. In the scripture reference James 2:26 "For as the body without the spirit is dead, so faith without works is also dead", at that very moment I have committed a vow to first put some work in my actions regarding to faith. You see, pleasing God happens when we have faith and apply it with action. The best solution for a trusting covenant with Him yes, you can say the marriage. I can tell you that in the testimony I shared with you my dear reader, remember I said that I was only working a part time job. Well to go a little deeper, I was only bringing home $198.00 dollars every other week. Although I had rental assistance, I still had to pay $400.00 dollars in rent, utilities, and car insurance and food. Just to say that in this time I never lacked in anything. The reason why was because I took the action in using my faith. God provided for my son and me and he is still providing lifelong provisions for my family and me to this day.

So, to you as the reader, please stay committed to your marriage with God regarding your faith and committed vow. Even when challenges arise, know that keeping the faith will carry us through. Remember the scripture tells us "Who shall separate us from the love of Christ? Shall trouble or hardship or persecution or famine, or nakedness or danger or sword? No, in all these we are more than conquerors through him who loved us." Romans 8:35-38.

Here are few simple tips of keeping the faith when difficulty is all around us:

- Lean into the faith that you have sometimes God is requiring you stretch a little more. Think of the discomfort while pushing forward as it builds endurance.

- Pray for strength and guidance. Lord, please order my steps in my faith walk that I may not take the detour to my will but your will.
- Remain focused and planted in Good Soil. In this, you surround yourself with those of like abilities and characteristics those I would call purpose pushers.

May the peace and favor of God continue to bless you in your marriage of faith and committed vow all the days of your life.

MICHELLE BOULDEN-HAMMOND

Biography

AUTHOR/LIFE COACH/MOTIVATIONAL SPEAKER/ PSALMIST

CREATING A REVOLUTION OF INSPIRATION

Michelle Boulden Hammond is a multitalented woman that handles her faith, marriage, business, and professional relationships with the power of inspirations. A small-town country girl from Talbot County, MD who has risen above life challenges from birth defect to low self-esteem, rejection, and mental abuse.

She received her Master of Arts in Human Services in Counseling from Liberty University and holds CLC Certificate from International Coaching Federation. Michelle with her charismatic personality has the power that gives individuals influence to move beyond their now. In her book called Seize the Moment to Inspire which was released October 2017, takes individuals on a 30day affirmation and meditation journey that is life changing. Her second book called "Little Girls Dreams Metamorphosis to Realities" was an anthology that brought some phenomenal women from all walks of life to share their dreams they had as little girls and now have brought them to realities as grown women.

Michelle also is a member of the BSN Black Speakers Network and in this capacity; she has hosted and traveled nationally and internationally for women empowerment conferences. In October 2018, she launched a group called TEAM M. A. B. B. (Mind, Affirmations, Beauty & Boldness). This group features four amazing women along with Michelle from the arenas of fashion, beauty and mental wellness. TEAM MABB will be conducting tours this coming year. Michelle's hosts yearly a women's retreat called Warm Your Heart, Warm Your Mind, Warm Your Soul which is a spiritual awakening women's empowerment retreat for mind, body and soul.

Testimonial "My first time at #WHWMWS Michelle's retreat ... I discovered who I really Am... Her motivational talk session called My Life Evaluator was great."

~Judith~

In Facebook Live Social Media, she has now opened her platform of IAM2Inspire TV which features weekly at 7pm Tuesdays weekly. She has received various awards for her community service and humanitarian efforts. In 2016, she was the first African American female in Talbot County, MD to open wellness center.

Topics

Personal Growth & Development

Life Skills

Holistic Health /Electromagnetic Therapy

Stress Management

Featured on

Ddtalks Radio Show

Women of Distinction Magazine

Co-Author of The Face of Adversity

MCTV

Forgiveness Nation

Website www.im2inspire.com

To have Michelle Boulden-Hammond featured in your city, please send booking inquiries to beinspired70@yahoo.com or contact number 410-253-6937.

RENEWING IN FAITH

By Ina Smith

RENEWING IN FAITH

By Ina Smith

Positioned in Faith

The meaning of flowing in faith is to capture the very depth of my recovery from major brain surgery back in 2000. At that time, I was 33 years old and a new mother to my son, Marcus. My son was born in July of 2000. Leading up to October 2000, I was weak, nauseated, and could not eat.

On the night of October 28, 2000, I returned home from dinner and a movie. At home, I spent over an hour vomiting in the bathroom. Afterwards, I requested to be taken to the Providence NE Hospital. During the ride, I sat in the backseat with my newborn. I held a bowl in my lap to vomit due to being so nauseated. Actually, I needed to be wheeled into the Emergency Room by a staff member. In the ER, I was given medications to control my vomiting and nausea. But, the vomiting and nausea continued and I needed to be admitted to the hospital. I was admitted on October 29, 2000. The Doctor diagnosed the symptoms being related to my Gallbladder. Therefore, I was scheduled for Gallbladder surgery on November 1, 2000. Ironically, I accepted Jesus as Lord on November 1, 1997. At the time I was 30 years old. Now, it's 3 years later and I am 33 years old. My newborn was 3-months old and he turned 4 months while I was in the hospital.

I was told that on the morning of October 31, 2000; the nurse found me disoriented and on the floor. At that time, I was scheduled for a CAT scan. The Cat Scan showed a bleed on my brain in the Cerebellum area. The medical terminology used for my Disability Paperwork was "Intracerebral Hemorrhage and Hematoma with Acute Hydrocephalus". In the meantime, to stop the bleed, a shunt and brain surgery was scheduled, and my Gallbladder surgery was cancelled.

Immediately, I was airlifted from Providence NE Hospital to Baptist Hospital for surgery.

A former church sister informed me that my "Last Rites" were administered on the helicopter. After 2010, I crossed paths with one of the nurses who prepared my body to be airlifted. I was in the store and the nurse recognized me. There was a surprise look on her face in disbelief.

Then, she stated, "We were thinking that she will not make it". At that time, my words laid still in my mouth because I had no memory.

I am grateful that God allowed me to cross paths with one of the nurses. Thus, the nurse comments, helps me to understand the depth of God, sparing my life. Thus, I would like my "Faith Story" to help detail God's healing power to impact, uplift, and encourage others.

Living in the Hospital Room in Faith

The brain surgery was a success, but the work was just beginning. In the hospital room, my days were spent pondering, "what happened?". I had many questions, but no one answered. Instead, my small frame laid a silent prisoner in my hospital room. In the daytime, I wheeled myself from my hospital room to the hallway with the other patients. My evenings were spent surrounded by walls and the television. I had my bible on the table near me for comfort. During this time, I was alone, thinking about life. I am sure my God was in the hospital room with me. His arms were holding and comforting me. I needed God's strength to endure the physical toil of what laid ahead. I needed faith to spur me out of the hospital room and the hospital forever.

In the hospital room, I grew accustomed to using "Bedpan." I dressed myself with help from the "Walker". At times, I would wheel, myself to the bathroom to check the mirror. I had to come to grips with my physical appearance. On one side of my head, I had my hair shaved due to the brain surgery. I had, an eye patch because my eyes were affected by the brain surgery. Then, my frame was under 100 pounds. I had help from the Occupational Therapist with the daily ritual of washing up in the bathroom. I took over these tasks, as my strength returned. The hospital room represented my limitations from the brain surgery, but my limitations were met by God's strengthening my faith.

Walking in Faith

The challenge of walking anew was beginning. Most of the mornings were spent in physical therapy. Afterwards, I returned to my room and cried due to the pain. Over a period of time, my tears were met with excitement. The results from physical therapy were very encouraging. I had to learn how to hold my body up. Then, I needed to strengthen my arms by learning how to catch a ball. I had to walk while holding onto a walker. This phase was followed by practicing, walking up makeshift stairs. Finally, I graduated to playing, hopscotch in the hallway. My faith strengthened due to my progression. I was no longer discouraged due to the strenuous work requirements. Suddenly I was getting stronger in body and mind. My faith was taking over. The tears were replaced with happiness. My hopes for discharge were approaching.

I was discharged on December 2, 2000. I continued, outpatient, my physical therapy, but experienced a setback. During outpatient physical therapy, my stomach pain recurred, Then, the pain prevented me from advancing in physical therapy. Again, I needed to have Gallbladder Surgery. Also, I needed to have a Tubal Ligation due to my diagnosis with Cardiomyopathy after my son was born. I requested that the two surgeries be performed on the same day. I did not want to be put under on two occasions. Afterwards the surgeries, I had a brief stay in the hospital. Afterwards, I resumed physical therapy with no other stomach problems. Today, I can reflect and thank God. The promotion from the pain was a kiss on my forehead from God. During the month of April 2001, I stopped using the wheelchair on a regular basis because of moments of weakness. At home, I enjoyed crawling and playing with my son. Then, I was promoted to being able to hold him, feed him, and just enjoy being a mother out of the confines of a wheelchair. As time passed, mothering was one of my biggest gifts from God. Today, my son is 20 years old and a sophomore in college. My daughter is approaching her senior year. I am a single mom and God in the name of Jesus my Lord has never left me from the hospital room in 2000 to walking there in 2021.

Speaking in Faith

My brain surgery resulted in me needing help with speaking. In the hospital, I had regular sessions with a Speech Therapist. I did not like speaking with the Speech Therapist. I recalled, the face cards to help me recite the words. On one visit, the Speech Therapist dialed my home answering machine and I heard my voice. Afterwards, the speaking improved with each session. My faith helped me to flow through the hardship of speaking anew. As I reflect, I realized that God had a plan for my voice. After being discharge, I returned back to being silent due to the accusatory spirits around me. In 2003, I removed myself from the toxic church environment.

In 2004, I self-published my book of Christian Poetry. At that time, I was more excited about being alive. My book became my ministry to share the power of God healing me from major brain surgery. Also, my book allowed me the opportunities to recite my poetry to an audience. I had the opportunity to be interviewed by

Dawn Mills Campbell on 95.3 FM radio station Then, another opportunity with Don Frierson at 620 AM radio station. Then, I was able to speak on two occasions in the Atlanta area. On one occasion, I had the opportunity to meet Mr. Larry Tinsley. I had the opportunity to give him a copy of my book. I hope that he read it in between interviewing famous gospel singers.

I was able to put my book in a consignment shop and a bookstore. Then, I was a part of a couple of local events. Finally, my book made it to Amazon. In 2004, this was a big deal for someone who almost died. Thus, I was not concerned about being a best seller or making a lot of money. Instead, I thought to myself, I want to leave an imprint on this earth with my book. All of these great opportunities may not have taken place without my faith flowing amidst the storm.

There was one fond moment that outshined me speaking at venues, being on the radio, and mailing my books to distant family and friends. I was most encouraged, by a former church sister. In 2004, Mary Jones called me because her co-workers wanted to buy a book. I met Mary and two of her co-workers at the "No Name Deli." Mary's co-worker started speaking about the Author. They stated, "She this." and "She that." Suddenly, Mary looked at me. She stated to her co-workers, "Ask the Author, she's right here." I was like, "What do you mean?" You see, my faith allowed me to write my experiences in poetry form. Thus, I was not prepared to share the work to others; it was my heart in writing.

Fighting and Writing in Faith

My writing started with self-publishing "My Inner Thoughts." I wrote thought provoking poems, honoring my relationship with my God, in the name of Jesus my Lord. Then, I shared my poem "Who I Am" in a poetry anthology. In the past, I worked with teenage males and females. I was honored to share and encourage God-provoking scriptures in "Walking with Her." Next, I read more poetry for the collaboration "Word Speaks." Finally, I shared my own story of healing in "Hush No More." First, Writers are impactful. Second, some Writers can be Healers. Third and finally, Jesus my Lord is the true Writer being the Author and Protector of my life.

Today, I realize that the storms can be brain surgery, a divorce, and other disappointments. I compare my faith to a boxing champion. As a faith champion, I must not allow the storms of life to knock me out. Instead, I must rise and just flow towards my God, in the name of Jesus my Lord. At the time of this writing entry, it is 2021 and I am still flowing in faith by writing. I am looking forward to my future writings and my imprint will live on through my writing.

INA SMITH

Biography

Ina Smith grew-up in the Capital Hill area of Washington, DC. Ina had the opportunity to earn an Associate Degree from Northern Virginia Community College in General Studies/Business, followed by a Bachelor's Degree in Health Care Administration from Marymount University. Ina completed her education by earning a Master's Degree in Social Administration from Case Western Reserve University. Currently, Ina works as a Licensed Masters Level Social Worker at the Department of Mental Health. She is completing a Certificate in Chaplaincy with Christ Central Ministries.

God has helped Ina to refocus on strengthening her relationship by being a part of several groups. These groups include Destiny's Walkers, Women N Power, Re-Discover Me, Glory

Carrier Women's Network, Issues In My Tissues (Prayer Line), The Growth Experience and Minister/Dr. Sharlene Mullings Prayer Ministry.

Ina is a self-published author of Christian Poetry, called "My Inner Thoughts." In addition, Ina is a part of two book collaborations, "Walk with Her" and "Hush No More." Also, she is part of a poetry anthology "Expression" and a book of poetry called "Words Speak."

Ina is a Deacon at her church. She has been on the past "Voice Committee". Currently, she is involved with the Health and Missions Ministries. She serves on the Nomination Committee. Ina loves reading and studying the bible. She continues to write and is revamping her writing ministry "Reveal Ministry. Ina is the mother to her son Marcus and her daughter Maya.

FAITH PHENOMENON

By Dr. Denise Victoria McAllister

FAITH PHENOMENON

By Dr. Denise Victoria McAllister

Before sharing one of many testimonies, I need to say: There are many stories and testimonies about my life that I have shared over the years. There is something incredibly significant about being a part of Flowing In Faith. I am grateful to have been selected to participate. Revelation knowledge can go a long way. Therefore, I needed guidance from God on what to share. I have no doubt that this story of Faith will touch everyone that will reads it.

What is Faith? Faith believes what we envision, pray for, and what we imagine will happen. Without a full explanation of how, when, or where. Sounds easy right? Keep reading.

The word phenomenon is defined as a fact or situation that is observed to exist or happen. Especially one whose cause or explanation is in question. Put these two words together and you have situations and circumstances that only the Almighty God can do. El Shaddai.

Here is one of my most recent episodes of Faith:

The years of 2012-2019 were the fieriest times of my life. I thought I had gone through the fire already many times. I discovered there are different levels of fire, which brings on different levels of the anointing. If we suffer with Christ, we will reign with Him. 2 Timothy 2:12

I was recovering from a traumatic car accident. Learning my new normal recovering from a spine injury and surgery. The Making of Mama Denise© I was getting to a place in my life to understand why God had allowed this too happened to me. Surely, He could have prevented this from happening.

Have you ever been in a place in life where you begin to ask God the question why me? Sure, you have. Only to find out later, it has all worked out for your good. If not, keep living and remember I said, "It will all work for your good." Romans 8:28

Life was different after the car accident in 2021. I managed to work an additional year from home during my recovery. In 2014, I could no longer endure the pain, and the memory of the car accident as well as the responsibility this position carried. I resigned (retired) from the best full-time, moneymaking, benefit-carrying government job; I believe I have ever had in my entire life, at that point. I just could not go any further. There were too many variables involved even though we needed the money.

Fortunately, the car accident case settled in my favor. I felt the settlement money I received would carry us through. I had received enough money to pay the mortgage at least for a year or more. I was still working part-time for a prestigious University as an Adjunct Professor. My husband was still working full time, so I felt we would be good financially. I was selling my Mama Denise© Cakes & Pies in a jar periodically and had speaking engagements so all is well. Looked like multi-streams of income to me.

I invested in some areas that I believed would bring in revenue to sustain us until I was well enough to go back to work. To me, I was in the perfect will of God. The pain was subsiding. The hospital marked my file Remarkable Recovery. I got through physical therapy with flying colors. Everything was going just as planned, so I thought. As a famous actor once said: "If you want to make God laugh, tell him about your plans."

Bills were being paid; food was in the refrigerator and on the shelf. Life was good. Until the investment did not go as I planned. My husband was laid off from his full-time job. The University where I was employed for over thirteen years dropped my position and the mortgage could no longer be paid. Didn't God know this was going to happen ahead of time? Why didn't He tell me? I have discovered - God is a strategist, we must trust Him.

Our finances and savings begin to deplete. Our refrigerator and the food pantry were bare. I am not one to whine or tell people what I am going through. I wait on God for direction of what to do. My phone was still ringing for people who needed prayer and direction in their lives. God would miraculously answer their prayers as I waited on the manifestation of mine.

My husband being the man he is began doing side jobs again going back to his initial job as a floor journeyman. His body at his age not being able to keep up as much as his younger years. He never complained and just kept going about it as a daily routine as if nothing were bothering him. I knew that this required more than natural ability. I knew we needed a Faith Phenomenon. A supernatural situation that would not be able to be explained except by four words "God Did It Again." This was a job for the "Queen of Faith." [*A name my BFF gave me a few years ago*] Sounds like some type of introductory music should be played right here for a superhero. I am no superhero. I just know Faith is a law and it works every time. I am what and who I am by the Grace of God.

I said, okay devil, we have been here before and I came out victorious. I have experienced these tests many times in my life. Where you as the enemy of my soul would want me to give up or cave in. I am not giving up and I am not caving in. I will fight with Faith, and I will win again. I Timothy 6:12

I do personal confessions every day. Prayer is my life. Praying, fasting, and confessions should always be in the mix. I even made one of my hallways during this time "A Hallway of Faith." I taped a Faith Confession on the wall eight times, and I would walk the hallway every morning saying "I am the Just, Therefore, I live by Faith – I walk by Faith – I believe in Faith – God is my source – God will never leave me or forsake me – My God Shall Supply "All" my

Need according to His Riches in Glory by Christ Jesus. I Believe God – The Blood of Jesus Prevails in and over my Life – I trust God. I added the Scripture "The scepter of the wicked will not remain over the land (houses) allotted to the righteous." Psalms 125:3a – adding my name for a direct spiritual connection. Every day for over eighteen months – I quoted this scripture repeatedly each day without missing one day.

As the days advanced, my home went into foreclosure. I still believed God for a turnaround. I was not looking at what I saw before me; I was looking at what the Word of God declared: "The scepter of the wicked will not remain over the land (houses) allotted to the righteous." I continued to be a tithes payer and a giver. God's Word declares I would be blessed and provided for – the devourer would be rebuked over my life and all nations will call me blessed. As Malachi 3:10-12 notes, I continued to stand on the promises of God.

Let me pause here, before I continue with the story. Was this easy to do? To continue to believe during a time of not knowing what would happen, of course not. You know why, it was not easy? We are human as well as divine. I was determined to make my spiritual woman stronger than anything my natural human self could ever achieve. I believe God and in Him is no darkness at all. I John 1:5. There is nothing missing, broken or damaged in the Kingdom of God and there will be nothing missing, broken or damaged in my life. This is where I live, and this is where I will stay.

My husband and I had been confessing we wanted to move to Florida for many years. I am not sure how many years we had been saying this – but it was prior to the car accident happening in my life. We would travel to Florida at least once a year on vacation to get the feel of the State. We would imagine what it would be like to live in Florida. *Golden Nugget: When we believe in something - never put the manifestation of what you believe for in a box. Thinking God must release the blessing in a certain way. Just keep on believing and confessing what you want to see. Nothing from God comes easy.* We have an adversary. I Peter 5:8 Do not be ignorant of the devil's devices. 2 Corinthians 2:11. The adversary will try to fight you every step of the way. Try to get you to panic. Try to get you to give up. Do not do it. Wait on God. He is faithful and He will see you through. Take on the full amour of God that you can resist the enemy and win. Ephesians 6:12-18.

Along the way you will also discover God has a tremendous sense of humor. Trust God and know His plans for us are good and not to do us evil. Jeremiah 29:11

As time went on, the bills were piling up. The gas bill, the electric bill, the water bill, the telephone bill. I was receiving negative mail from my mortgage company, almost every day. I prayed over those envelopes, wrote scriptures on them, and put across the front Paid in Full in Jesus Name. I also added what I believed for to my Vision Boards.

I was offered to have a meeting with the mortgage company and the State's Administration Office to try to work out a plan to repay or catch up my mortgage. I was eligible to file for refinance. Unfortunately, every time I applied it was rejected because my husband nor I made enough money to show we would be able to afford to pay the mortgage monthly. This was no time to stop believing. The day I was scheduled to meet with the mortgage company's attorney and the State's Administration Department there was a terrific snowstorm, and the meeting was postponed for two weeks. I was never so happy to see snow before in my life. God had given me more time to believe and wait for the manifestation. Then the date was getting closer for the new meeting. All I could do was to continue to have Faith to believe for a financial miracle. Walking the "Hall of Faith" in my house and believing for a miracle. I continue to sow and pay my tithes out of whatever came in. Matthew 18:19, Luke 6:38, Malachi 3:10-12

As I begin to look into the spirit realm, I could see the Favor of God. Many individuals are not allowed to go the length of time as I did – owing a significant amount of back mortgage payments - without being evicted. God was at work on my behalf and I knew it. I just did not know how, when or where the blessing would come. I believed this situation was not unto devastation; it was unto God being glorified.

The house was completely in my name – therefore, I was the sole responsible party for this debt. There was some type of new law that was passed in 2018 that you could not use the income of your spouse or anyone living in the home with you if they were not on the initial Deed. It was a few days before I was supposed to have the meeting with the mortgage attorney and the State Administration Officer. It just so happened that a monumental former President of the United States died that same week; and the day of his funeral was made a Federal Holiday. This was same day we were supposed to meet and Federal offices were closed. Another miracle of favor. God gave me more time. I had another two weeks to see what was going to happen next. Glory to God.

Finally, the time came to have the meeting. By now, I had been offered a management job with an individual who owned his own business and had been coined a Multi-Millionaire. He asked me to become his Project Manager in a new venture he was putting together. My salary would be almost identical to what I was making with the Federal Government. I used that information at the mortgage meeting to inform them I had been promised employment and the starting date offered to me. The State's Administrator and the mortgage attorney afforded me a couple more weeks to put all this in place. Favor! The starting date and salary met the requirements to either bring the mortgage current, make partial payments, or qualify for refinance. Thank you, Jesus.

Well, guess what? None of that happened. The guy I was supposed to work with seemed to be suffering from some type of psychological disorder. I found out his finances had been depleted long before he offered me the job, due to bad investments. His wife had left him, and he was amid a divorce. He was only making about $37,000 a year through a former investment partner he was helping. Jesus take the wheel. Now what?

Even though my flesh seems to be getting weak, my spirit was strong. I continued to walk the Hall of Faith in my house. Praying, Confessing and Believing. I knew God would come through for me. God gave me a song during this – I do not know how you are going to do it, but I know you can, and you will. Thank God for my husband's support and his prayers during this time. When I was feeling weak, he was strong and vice versa. Two are better than one. Ecclesiastes 4:9-12

Watching television one day, I saw a commercial where a company could help sell my house in a few days. The Holy Spirit said call them. I received in my spirit it was time to sell the house. It was time to move to Florida. God knows the end from the beginning. Isaiah 46:10 I contacted the company that same day and was told I was too far into the foreclosure and they could not help me. I was then referred to someone else who could possibly help me. I called this number and had to leave a voicemail. I waited for about two days and then called again. Someone answered. I spoke with the man that answered the phone and explained my situation. I said, unashamedly, I hope you do not mind me mentioning God; I am hoping for a miracle. He said back to me; I am a minister and asked could he pray for me. I immediately started crying tears of joy. God had sent me help. He is never late – He is right on time.

This man was a broker and a realtor and gave me explicit instructions what to do. That part of the story is entirely another chapter. This process was horrific to say the least. From having to go to the United States Foreclosure office several times, filing documents, meetings, and talking with attorneys. Up late at night, trying to figure out what to do. How to do. Asking myself the question is any of this working? Will it work? Where is God?

I remember finally standing before the Judge who had to make a decision that would change the course of me losing my house or selling it. I fought back the tears as I stood before him. Matthew 10:19. The final analysis - my house was sold for more than what I owed. Foreclosure was removed without prejudice. We were able to pay off the house and have enough money to hire professional packers and a moving company to move to Florida. We had more than enough money to live on until God gave us our jobs. This was Faith Phenomenon - unexplainable. God did it again. God never ceases to amaze me. Trust God and you will see that you mean everything to Him. You will experience the Love of God right before your eyes. His ways are beyond what we could ever imagine or think. The blessings do not always come in a wrapped package with a bow on them. They often come through the valley of the shadow of death, but know God is with us. Faith Phenomenon will happen if we just believe.

DR. DENISE VICTORIA MCALLISTER

Biography

Dr. Denise Victoria McAllister was born in Jersey City, New Jersey raised in Newark, New Jersey. She has resided in the State of Maryland for the past eighteen years. In 2019, Dr. McAllister relocated to the Central Florida Region. She is a national and international speaker having traveled across country and overseas.

Dr. McAllister served as an Advanced Certified Faculty member for the University of Phoenix teaching classes in Behavioral Science and Psychology for eleven years. She was conferred a Doctorate in Philosophy in Biblical Counseling through Friends International Christian University, Merced, California. Her dissertation to receive her doctorate is entitled: The Incarceration of Women with and Without Walls. She has a Master of Social Sciences in Professional Counseling from Grand Canyon

University, Phoenix, Arizona and a Master of Theology from Drew University, Madison, New Jersey

Dr. McAllister is an accomplished author of several books:

- The Making of Mama Denise©
- *Co-Author* of Flowing In Faith©
- Book of Remembrance -Miracle, They Really Do Happen©
- He Heard My Cry©
- Dreams, A LifeSaver Kept Me Alive©

Dr. (Shipley) McAllister made history becoming the first African American Woman Chaplain over the Newark, New Jersey Police Department receiving Deputy Chief Rank in 1995. This event was featured on Channel 9 News and in the Newspapers.

Dr. McAllister has received numerous awards and citations over the years. A few notable mentions are:

- US Military Moving Specialist Designation
- Featured in O Magazine - Oprah Winfrey's Publication
- Ordained Licensed Minister
- Charles County, Maryland – Volunteer Award for NAACP
- Board Advisor, Hope Center, Clermont, Florida

- Care Counselor, Hope Center, Clermont, Florida
- Nominated Outstanding Employee, Walter Reed National Military Medical Center, Bethesda, Maryland
- Notary Public, State of Florida

Dr. Denise McAllister owns and operations Mama Denise© Cakes & Pies in a Jar; officially Trademark under the United States in the bakery industry. Dr McAllister's desire in life is to let the world know that when we have Faith coupled with belief in ourselves, we can do, be and have anything we desire. Dr. Denise Victoria McAllister has been married to Anthony Dwight McAllister for the past twenty-three years as of this writing. They have four children together and eight grandchildren. For more information or to contact Dr McAllister visit www.successful1.net

GOD'S PRESENCE IN THE MIDST OF THE UNTHINKABLE

By Debra Thornton

GOD'S PRESENCE IN THE MIDST OF THE UNTHINKABLE

By Debra Thornton

Many years ago, there was a skinny little girl with piercing brown eyes, who smiled shyly on the outside. But, behind the shy smile and piercing brown eyes was a terrible secret. You see, several members of her extended family were molesting her. She shared this secret with no one; not even her parents until she was a grown woman. For many years, she thought she was to blame for what was done to her. This violation produced years of shame, depression, sadness, and anger. Because she was young, she did not have the necessary skills to process this trauma. She blamed herself for what happened and in her mind, it had to be her fault. What followed were years of perfectionism, and people pleasing. In fact, she became the ultimate people pleaser. She became a walking robot, doing everything and trying to be everything she thought others wanted her to be.

Although she carried this terrible secret inside, she accomplished many things in her life, including earning both undergraduate and graduate degrees and establishing a successful career in finance. Even with all the love, support, and many accolades from her family and friends, there was still the underlying shame, sadness, and general feeling of not measuring up.

That little girl was me and this is the first time I have ever shared this publicly. In fact, it was not until I was in my late twenties that I actually verbalized what happened to me and shared part of my secret with a relative. A couple of years before I shared my story, I had become a Christian. In my naivety, I thought when I became a Christian; I would not have to deal with this part of my life. I focused on becoming the "perfect" Christian, by attending every service, every church function, and being part of every church ministry. There is nothing wrong with these actions, but I was doing it because I was running from my life.

Slowly, Jesus began pulling back the layers and He gave me the courage to face this awful secret. God gave me the courage to tell my parents who have been supportive while navigating their own anger and sadness. God gave me the courage to face my abusers who apologized. God also gave me the courage to begin therapy to unpack the trauma in a safe environment. One of things I learned in therapy, is when someone is violated this way; it touches the most intimate part of their soul. It affected me in many ways. To this day, I cannot sleep in a very dark room. I am easily startled by the simplest noise of someone tapping on a wall or walking up to me from behind. I also unconsciously developed dysfunctional ways to manage my emotions, and unhealthy coping skills of overcompensating. God showed me that during my darkest times, He was there.

You see, I know He was there, because I am still here. During my times of depression, I could have ended my life. Many times, I considered it, but God in his mercy did not allow me to. Because He had a purpose for my life and for my pain. Romans 8:28 says, "And we know that all things work together for good to them that love God, to them who are the called according to his purpose" (KJV). You see, God did not cause what happened to me, but because I love God, He has used it for good.

You are probably asking, "What good could have possibly come from something so awful?" I am glad you asked. First, it has brought me closer to Jesus. It is still bringing me closer to Jesus. You see, the prophet Isaiah in Isaiah 53:3 speaks of Jesus being acquainted with our griefs. That same prophet also speaks of Jesus bearing our griefs and sorrows. If no one understands what I went through, Jesus understands. Jesus demonstrated this by dying for my sins. I also see that He orchestrated events in my life to bring me closer to Him, and He led me to people who could walk with me through this journey.

Secondly, it brought my family and I closer together. My parents had no idea what was going on. Even while working through their own feelings, they continue to support me during my healing. I remember my mother saying when I told her, "Now I understand why you acted certain ways and did certain things." My father has also been supportive during my healing journey.

If you are reading this, and you are a sexual abuse survivor, please consider these steps:

1. If you have never accepted the forgiveness that God gives through the sacrifice of His son Jesus, please do that now. Romans 10:9 says, "If you declare with your mouth, "Jesus is Lord," and believe in your heart that God raised him from the dead, you will be saved." Pray this simple prayer: "Dear Lord Jesus, I know that I am a sinner, and I ask for Your forgiveness. I believe You died for my sins and rose from the dead. I turn

from my sins and invite You to come into my heart and life. I want to trust and follow You as my Lord and Savior." If you have prayed that prayer, I want to be the first to say, "Welcome to the Kingdom!"

2. Share your story with someone who you trust. It could be a friend, a relative, or a Pastor. This will help you begin the process of healing. You can also write it out in a journal. I will go into this later.

3. Find a good Christian therapist who has experience in the area of sexual abuse and trauma. Make sure you feel comfortable and safe with the person you choose. I recognize that some Christian circles do not embrace the idea of therapy, but I strongly encourage you to step out of your comfort zone and seek help. I struggled with the idea of needing therapy and being a Christian too, but I realized that therapists are highly trained to deal with those who have been affected with this trauma. Ask yourself this question: "If I break my arm, would I go to the doctor?" Of course, you would. Well, your mind, emotions, and soul are broken, and in the need of repairing. Therapy along with Jesus is crucial.

4. Buy yourself a nice journal to write your thoughts, prayers, and feelings. Do not worry about correct grammar; just write whatever comes to your mind. Some of your thoughts and feelings will be raw. Do not be afraid of the rawness of your thoughts. You will find it very therapeutic to get them out of your head and onto the paper. Journaling has been instrumental in my healing. I use my journal to write down my thoughts and prayers. Sometimes, when I am having trouble praying aloud, I find writing my prayers to God helps me. I also use it write down scriptures that speak to me when I am reading my Bible.

5. Be gentle with yourself. Everyone's healing period is unique to them. I am an accountant, which means, everything I do in my profession must add up to a bottomline number. It also means that I think in terms of black and white. I tend to approach every situation the same way an accountant approaches a financial statement. In my world, 1 + 1 must equal 2. It cannot equal 3. Unfortunately, when healing from the damage of sexual abuse, everything will not add up nicely or be tied into a neat bow. Healing takes time. Give yourself grace. God is with you. At times, the healing journey will be messy, but it will be worth it.

6. This last step may be the hardest, but it is the most freeing. It is forgiveness. Let me say that again, it is forgiveness. This was the hardest for me to do. In fact, I will be very transparent and say that I only truly forgave the people involved 4 days ago. When I sat down to write, God through a series of events reminded me that I had not completed this step. Forgiveness means that you do not hold the offense against the person anymore. However, let me be clear, forgiveness does not mean you are giving them a pass. It means you are allowing the bitterness to leave your soul. Please understand this: forgiveness does NOT mean you have to allow that person to be a part of your life. In fact, although I have forgiven the people involved, I choose not to allow them to be a part of my life. The decision is up to you to determine the offender's level of involvement in your life.

I would like to end by saying that I am still a work in process. If you had asked me a year ago to tell my story publicly, my answer would have been an unequivocal NO! I guess God has a sense of humor. Just know, I am still doing my work. I am not perfect, nor have I arrived. I still have questions that may not be answered until I am in heaven. However, it is okay. God is still faithful, and He is using the worst pain in my life for His purpose.

DEBRA THORNTON

Biography

Debra Thornton accepted Christ as her Lord and Savior on March 13, 1994. She could not anticipate in her wildest dreams, the incredible journey she was embarking on with this decision. While naturally introverted, God has slowly given her the courage to share her story and voice with the world and embrace her God given identity.

As a Financial Management Professional, Debra holds a Bachelor of Arts Degree in Accounting (Immaculata University) and a Master of Arts Degree in Management (Notre Dame University of Maryland). Debra is active in her church where she currently serves as a Greeter, and a Facilitator for Financial Peace University.

In her spare time, Ms. Thornton loves traveling to Sedona, Arizona, Disney World, Dallas, Texas, cruising to exotic Caribbean Islands, and spending time with her family and friends. A native of Maryland, Debra loves collecting anything purple, and indulging in her favorite past time of baking mouth-watering Southern Style cakes.

Contact Information:

Cell: (443) 312-9338

Email: Toopurple4u@gmail.com

MAKING OF A DIAMOND THROUGH FAITH

By Dr. Astril Webb

MAKING OF A DIAMOND THROUGH FAITH

By Dr. Astril Webb

As a believer in the Lord Jesus Christ, have you ever really looked back on your life and counted all the ways God has blessed you? Do not just think about the BIG wins but the smallest blessings like having electricity in your home, and trash pick-up services in your neighborhood. The knowledge that the sun rises and sets every day even on a rainy day or knowing that water flows in the lowest parts of the forest helps us through our days. Sometimes we focus on abundance, but the blessings are also in the smallest details, the trials, and the difficulties of life.

In retrospect, I can reflect on the love, mercy, and grace of God over my lifetime. There are people who I have been blessed to know and I am thankful for the lessons revealed through hardships and those who stood against me. The adversities and trials in life were ultimately in God's plan for me and there were valuable lessons learned. I am a witness that truly everything works together for our good, as the Lord promised, if we only learn to live by FAITH and not by sight.

You see, I never knew that my journey as a baby from the beautiful Caribbean islands of Trinidad and Tobago, born to a mother of East Indian descent and father of African heritage, would lead me to migrate to the United States. I became a medical doctor and married my best friend. I am a mother of two amazing miracle babies and have influenced the healthcare industry as a change agent. I have travelled to 22 states within the United States and 12 countries around the world. I became a recognized community leader by President Obama's Council on Fitness, Sports and Nutrition, and rose as a Global Change Agent, Trainer and Public Speaker.

Although many can view my successes as significant accomplishments, I recognize them as the rewards for beholding unwavering faith in my Lord in each season of life. In 2013, something appeared to be missing, despite achieving impressive milestones, and I knew I was lacking something. I felt God was calling me to do more. More you say. Yes, more. In midOctober, around 4:30am on a Thursday, I was awakened by a loud audible voice calling my name twice *"Astril, Astril."* The sound was mighty and sounded like the roaring sea. At first, I thought it was my husband, but he was laying fast asleep next to me. I sat up in bed wondering if I was dreaming. "*But the voice was so clear*", I thought. I asked God if it was Him. There was no immediate answer. Days later, I realized, and to this day still convinced, that I heard the voice of God. Since then, my hunger to learn from the scriptures grew and I felt the inclination to move away from the busyness of life to quiet my spirit and move from healthcare into health ministry.

As a child growing up in a Christian home in Trinidad, I was exposed to the gospel of grace and witnessed how my parents lived by faith, depending, and trusting the Lord for everything. At the age of 12, I personally asked Jesus to enter my heart to be my Lord and Savior and change me for His plan and purpose. I was water baptized to declare my faith and lived my life trusting the Lord. During my senior high school year, I prayed that if God would not allow me to attend medical school, then I would consider entering the ministry. God had a plan and led me to pursue my medical career. The journey did not come without financial challenges and hardships at Howard University in Washington DC. God always provided, even when others doubted and questioned my belief that God would make a way. I am grateful for my parents and siblings who supported me and the handful of friends who believed in me and encouraged me.

I successfully completed my medical training in Germany, and this changed the trajectory of my future. Embracing a new culture, being the first person of color to work in the hospital there, undergoing many experiences of racism by patients and non-physician staff members, *yet* professionally accepted by close colleagues. Being "*adopted*" by my German family "*The Gockels*" and their close circle of family and friends, added to my blended experiences. These were the lessons and blessings gifted to me then that eventually prepared me for my current life's work.

After having two miracle babies, *(who could have been severely disabled according to medical standards if not for God's grace)*; two major car accidents within 5 months in 2016, which caused me to be confined to bed for 8 months and having physical therapy three times a week due to severe neck and back injuries; these were very challenging times. Contracts for my own business were lost due to physical limitations. Later in March 2020, I lost all my training contracts due to the invisible COVID-19 virus and not a moment goes by when I cannot declare the GOODNESS OF GOD. Living by faith involves embracing humility, trials, and challenges, not just the good things. It is only then when we are faced with uncertainty, crossroads, and extreme storms of life that God can reveal his complete wholeness, healing, provision, and protection because we have no choice but to trust Him to do the impossible.

Think about the making of diamonds for a moment. These precious stones are made from pure carbon atoms under tremendous pressure and harshest conditions. At the end, we observe a complete perfect masterpiece that shows magnificence and brilliance. In fact, diamonds are the hardest compounds found on the earth today. Similarly, when we trust God's plan and accept the trials and pressures of life as part of the process, to strengthen our character and dependency on the Holy Spirit, the Glory and Goodness of God will be revealed in our situations. Jesus as the author and finisher of our faith will shine in our work, our lives, and all we do. The blessings are truly not from our own efforts but from the unconditional love, abundance of grace, and the favor of our Lord.

Honestly, I have never been so blessed in all my life. I embrace the peace, joy and righteousness of Christ seeking first the Kingdom of God and ALL things that matter have been added unto me. Matthew 6:33. I no longer live by sight, only by faith. You see my faith flows when there is no other possibility, and there is nothing else I can do BUT stand on God's word and promises. He is ever present with you and me.

Each season of my life was ordered by my Heavenly Father. The hard lessons and periods in the wilderness were necessary to prepare me for all God has deemed for me on this earth. If it had not been for the leaps of Faith to TRUST God with all my heart and lean not on my own understanding in my past, I would have never experienced my stance today. Unmovable, unwavering faith in my Lord while prayerfully remaining patient during the process.

God has taken me places I could never have imagined. I stand humbled as a child of God. His grace has sustained me through all the accidents, sickness, hardships, lack, prejudice, and uncertainties of life. I developed and implemented many health and wellness initiatives, trained thousands of people ultimately impacting 9 million lives over the years in healthcare, had the honor to expose my work to Presidents, Prime Ministers, Ambassadors, Beauty Queens, Secretaries of multiple Government Agencies, senior executives, business owners, nonprofits, faith-based communities, and social organizations. I believe this is just the beginning and eyes have not yet seen all that God has for me.

All the GLORY belongs to Christ alone. I am so very thankful that God uses me as a vessel to serve others and in return, I have received the multitude of blessings and favor in my life. My success is not defined by man nor is it measured according to man's standards. The fulfilment in my life has been truly dependent on the unearned, unmerited favor of God through Christ Jesus. His grace, mercy, and never-ending love and kindness towards me is what everyone sees. They do not know about the tears, pain, setbacks, criticisms, unkind comments, and rejections I had to endure along the way.

Each person has a story, and if we are honest, we recognize countless blessings from a loving Heavenly Father and Savior who never leave nor forsake us. I would live this life all over again the same way knowing what I know now. God's grace through Christ Jesus is more than sufficient for me.

Here are five wisdom pearls I wish to leave with you:

1. Freely recognize that God loves you and has an amazing plan for your life. Open your heart to Jesus, allow the Holy Spirit to guide you always, and search for Him in the scriptures.
2. Adversity as an opportunity that allows you to stay in fervent prayer. Be thankful in every season of your life.
3. In tough times, lean not on your own understanding. There are questions that you will have concerning your circumstances

but choose to see all things as either blessings or lessons. Trust His timing and His plan.

4. The devil will try to distract you from the BEST God has for you. Living by FAITH will not come without challenges. Faith is the KEY to unlocking your success. Believe and stand on the Word of God.
5. Having done all you can, BE STILL and know that God will turn around things for your good and he will reward you for your steadfast faith because of the finished work of Christ.

God bless you!

Dedicated to: Dr. Lloyd Webb, The Late Margaret Webb, Dixie, Lyndon, Lecarde, Mike, Lesalle, Soleila, The Gockels, Howard U. Crew, family & friends.

DR. ASTRIL WEBB

Biography

Dr. Astril Webb is a Senior Healthcare Professional, Global Trainer, Public Speaker and Human Rights Consultant with over two decades of senior level experience. She founded *Healthy Kinder International, LLC* and as President, has developed and implemented effective culturally competent health promotion and prevention coaching and training programs in the US, Caribbean, Europe, and Africa. With profound expertise in eliminating health disparities and passion to address preventable health issues, she has spearheaded many initiatives under healthcare and health ministry and has presented at numerous national and international conferences. As a Global Speaker, Dr. Webb has participated at International Women's Day events and Global Summits contributing to Women's and Girls Rights to Health and Mental

Health services and advocacy against health inequality and systemic racism.

In April 2014, she was honored with the *distinguished President Obama's Council on Fitness, Sports & Nutrition Community Leadership Award*, for exemplary service and dedication to improving the health and lives of others making a significant impact in public health. She is dual-certified as a Youth and Adult Mental Health First Aid USA instructor. She attributes her successful impact to her calling, unconditional love and support from her family and friends and experiences drawn from vulnerable medical communities.

Contact

Email: HKIPresident@gmail.com

Website: https://www.healthykinder.org

Facebook @healthykinderinternational

LinkedIn Dr. Astril Webb

FAITH ALWAYS BRINGS VICTORY

By Bernadette M Brawner

FAITH ALWAYS BRINGS VICTORY

By Bernadette M Brawner

Initially when the Lord placed on my heart to do a book anthology on faith, the story that I wanted to share was replaced with this one. You see, we all have experienced a fiery test, at some point in our lives and if you have not please brace yourself. In fact, as Christians, we should expect to be tested. While we do not like to be tested, it is the only way we grow in Christ. It does not matter how young or old you are, but how you handle the wave. You have a choice to hold unto God's unchanging hand, trust Him by faith or we can be like a rocking chair moving back and forth but going nowhere, also known as worrying. Faith moves with action, even when we are afraid. We keep moving because we know & trust that God is with us every step of the way.

How many of you would agree that 2020, the new decade, came with great expectancy and new beginnings? Yes, I did too. I had promised myself that this was the year that I was going to execute what I wrote as my goals in January but by March 2020, these plans came to a halt due to the worldwide pandemic. While I have encountered many blessings this year between January and July to include an opportunity for professional development, being granted to work from home full-time, receiving unexpected checks in the mail, multiple job interviews and offers, to starting a new job exactly 11 years later the same day. I also was faced with a situation that rocked me to my core. I was sailing through this year on cloud nine. Thankful and grateful for every blessing that was given to me. Then, I hit some deep waves and was faced with a test that made me hold on to my faith with all that I had within me.

On August 27, 2020, I had two missed calls from my daughter. My initial thought was that she needed me to pay for her doctor's co-payment. I called her back. When she picked up the call, her voice was low and faint. I heard her say "mommy", but her voice sounded different and raised my concerned. I asked her what was wrong, and she answered, the doctor thinks that I have CANCER. My life changed almost instantly, my heart dropped, and I immediately went into prayer mode. She was very emotional and crying. I was home and she was about 20 miles away and I wanted to go and be with her, but she said that she would be ok driving home by herself.

My brain stopped working and felt shattered. I began pacing the floor and rehearsing in my head what I had just heard. I was quoting this scripture to remind myself of who I was in Christ and that God is with me, "For we walk by faith, not by sight." This was all I could muster up while I waited for my daughter to come home. I prayed, cried, and asked God to keep me strong for my child. I could not understand how and why the doctor thought she might have cancer. In our minds, she was experiencing allergic reactions to her fur baby, Zeus, but this could be fixed with a steroid. Cancer never crossed our minds, especially since she has never been sick before. In fact, she had her physical in January and got a clean bill of health. How could this happen? At this point, I was nervous, nauseous, and anxious. I guess you could say, I was an emotional wreck. All I wanted to do was see my child. I kept looking out the window in anticipation of her pulling up to the house. The 30-minute ride felt like eternity for her to get home. As soon as I saw her pull up in the driveway, I ran to the door, our eyes locked, and our tears flowed uncontrollable as I grabbed and held her so tight.

I guess you can say that we were in shock and disbelief of the possibility of cancer running in our family again. No one wanted to say what we were all thinking, but it came out when the family started discussing the possibility of my daughter having this illness. In January 2013, my mom passed away from brain cancer and we were devastated. We lost our matriarch. Why are we dealing with this again seven years later? How many of you know that God had a plan for us? The scriptures tell us in Jeremiah 29:11, "For I know the thoughts that I think toward you, says the LORD, thoughts of peace and not of evil, to give you a future and a hope."

After we got ourselves together, we calmly sat in silence for about an hour. Then my daughter said, "Can you call all of your prayer warriors and ask them to pray for me?" I was going to reach out to my prayer warriors, but what surprised me was she had asked for their prayers. Normally, I was looked upon as a holy roller, but this day, mine and other holy roller prayers were selected. I believe that she knew that when we prayed, God heard our petitions. Even during this time of sadness, this request warmed my heart. I had been praying since 2018 to reconcile her back unto God. I thought that she had forgotten all about the principles and precepts she had learned growing up in the church and at home. I was honored to know that she realized that I am connected to God and was no longer embarrassed by the relationship that I had with Christ. This was the first sign of God's plan in her life. Can I tell you that within two weeks I saw a transformation in my child that only the true and living God could do?

God prepared my daughter for what she was about to face and this caterpillar metalloid into a butterfly. So now, we are in September and these life events were overwhelming and hard to digest. My anxiety increased as well as my prayer life. I started a new job and while this was a happy occasion, it was hard to celebrate. The doctor finally called and confirmed our worst fear, and it had a name. The type of cancer that she was diagnosed with is a blood disease, Hodgkin's Lymphoma. So, what exactly is Hodgkin's Lymphoma and how did she get this disease? Well, Hodgkin's lymphoma — formerly known as Hodgkin's disease — is a cancer of the lymphatic system, which is part of your immune system. It may affect people of any age but is most common in people between 20 and 40 years old and those over 55. The doctor said it is not known how one gets this disease.

To give you insight on what we were told by the Oncologist, I will describe as much as possible about the diagnosis. Let us start with the initial CAT scan in early August. At this time, the mass measured about 5.5 cm. The doctor took pictures of the lymph nodes on her neck and saw something in her chest. The next order was for her to get a CT scan of her chest to find out what was going on in this part of her body. The mass in her chest measured 6.3 cm and appeared to be growing at a rapid rate as well as pressing on a main artery, her airwaves. The medical term is trachea. We found out that she was at Stage 2 of this illness. We were told that her Erythrocyte Sedimentation rate (ESR) was elevated to 60, which is an inflammatory marker indicating that this cancer is aggressive. Lastly, the doctor explained that this type of cancer is curable, but her treatment plan must be aggressive and chemo infusion needed to start in the coming weeks.

Another issue that had to be considered is whether she will be able to have children. It is a possibility that after chemotherapy, she may not be able to have children. My daughter had to decide at the tender age of 24 on whether to save her life and possibly not have children after this treatment plan was over or see a fertility doctor to save her eggs and risk the chance of this aggressive cancer to overtake her body. I will tell you that receiving this information was very overwhelming. As we sat in the patient room listening to the doctor explain all of this to us, we felt lost and numb. All I could utter is God, please save my child. Now my faith is being tested and had to hold tightly onto my faith. I was reminded of 1 Corinthians 15:58, which states,

"Therefore, my beloved brethren, be steadfast, immovable, always abounding in the work of the Lord, knowing that your labor is not in vain in the Lord."

Now that we have the diagnosis, the doctors also revealed that her case was severe, and her treatment plan will be accelerated. She decided to save her life first and pray that after all this is over, God would continue to bless her, and infertility will not be an issue. Her treatment plan was to get a port placed in her chest and chemo infusions every two weeks. Once we got home from the doctor's office, we had to let all this information sink in and get ready for our new normal. On October 12, 2020, she had surgery to get port placed in her chest. Then chemo infusions started three days later. Anyone that has taken care of a loved one with a critical illness knows this is not an easy feat. I felt helpless and for the first time in my life, I did not know how to care for my child. I cried out to God for direction. A few days after the first infusion, she became extremely weak and could not eat. All she had energy enough to do is sleep and go to the bathroom. This treatment was an energy zapper. I could not sleep and found myself waking up every hour to go check on her to make sure she was breathing. This reminded me of when she was first born. I know I am not the only parent that used to check on their newborn baby. Well now, my newborn baby is 24 years old. I prayed for strength, grace, and hope to keep believing that God was going to keep me strong during this fiery test and He was going to heal my child.

Over the next two months, we were on a rollercoaster ride. My daughter found out that she had developed blood clots in each arm and in her juggler vein. There were trips to the emergency room. Our emotions were on high every day and night. I am so glad that we have a strong prayer life; family and friends that lift us in prayer. Our faith community is strong, and their prayers were felt and changed things. When going through deep waters or a test, we must find a scripture to hold onto to keep us from giving up. Well, by the time my daughter went to her next doctor's appointment, she found out that the blood clots in her arms were gone, yes gone. Not only that, but the blood clot on the juggler vein had also opened and blood was flowing through her veins. We said that that was the blood of the Lord! The doctor and assistant were in shock. They said that they had never seen anything like this before. We knew exactly what had happen. God did that!

We needed this good news after months of lows and dealing with this illness, things were turning around. Next, my daughter had to get a second pet scan to check on the progress of the cancer. Let me tell you my faith in God grew intensely as if I have wrapped myself around Jesus Himself. I was intentional about my faith because this is all I had to truly keep me from losing hope. A dear friend of mine and co-author in this book, Dr. Victoria McAllister, blessed me with a scripture that I used during this difficult time of caring for my child. The scripture is Matthew 15:28 - Then Jesus answered and said to her, "O woman, great *is* your faith! Let it be to you as you desire." And, her daughter was healed from that very hour. I know that my daughter is already healed. I believe we must endure and go through the process to get to the victory also known as the promises of God. 1 John 5:4 – "For whatever is born of God overcomes the world; and this is the victory that has overcome the world—**our faith**." Now this process is not over, but we have the faith that God has already healed her body.

Can someone say there is more good news to share? Yes, I would like to share that we received a good report after my daughter's pet scan in December. She learned that her cancer was 90% gone and she is responding well to the treatment. She must continue with chemo infusions for the next couple of months. The doctors want to ensure that all the cancer is gone and that her body would start producing new cells. So, what does this mean? I am happy to explain. The large mass in her chest and the others around her heart and trachea are gone. Praise Break! Come on and shout with me... HALLELUJAH!!!!!!! We screamed, cried, shouted, and thanked our heavenly Father. Our hearts are filled with gratefulness. We never stopped believing that our God is faithful. In closing, I am encouraging each reader to keep the faith no matter what fiery test that you will encounter. Remember that God has you and will never forsake you if you believe.

Proverbs 2:7-8 – He holds VICTORY in store for the upright and protects the way of the FAITHFUL

Psalm 34:17 - The righteous cry out and the LORD hears them; he delivers them from all their troubles

Remember to act **by FAITH**:

F – ollow

A – bide

I – mplore (pray)

T – rust in

H – im (Christ Jesus)

BERNADETTE BRAWNER

Biography

As Chief Executive Officer of BB Coaching and Consulting, Bernadette's personal and professional life has exemplified the powerful result of what happens when an individual perseveres, strives for more, and consistently moves forward despite their circumstances. She went from experiencing many challenges when it came to her journey and her purpose to reaching great heights professionally; working for the federal government and doing over 45 trainings over these past 29 years to continue to soar to even greater heights. Personally, her confidence and strength has grown and evolved to the point where she now empowers others through BB Coaching and Consulting and her nonprofit organization, Sisters Helping Empower Each Other (SHEE). As a single mother, despite the odds against her, she was able to raise a daughter who she has an unbelievable relationship with; one of the victories she acknowledges as one of her greatest achievements.

As a Certified Life Coach, Bernadette also holds a Master of Business Administration (MBA) degree and a background that allows her to create impact on the systems and strategic direction of her clients. She is a facilitator, motivational speaker, and a community volunteer. For the past three years, Bernadette has served as a Facilitator for the **Atlanta Glow** Leadership of Women Organization, Life Skills Program, speaking in the areas of "Made with Love" self-care workshop and "Healthy Relationships" workshop to women ages 18 -28.

She loves volunteering regularly with her church, Impact Once church, **Each One Feed One, Inc. (EOFO)** to feed & provide resources to the homeless. Her nonprofit organization, **Strength Hope Encouragement and Empowerment - S.H.E.E.**, has also in the past, partnered with the **Craig Shields Foundation** to provide backpacks and school supplies to the local community. Ms. Brawner is an active member of multiple Toastmaster International Clubs and is the immediate past President of the Federal Triangle Toastmasters Club. She served as a Board Member with I Am Who I Am Corporation and a tutor for Charles County Literacy Council.

Ms. Brawner is the author of a 31-day revival prayer devotional, **Strength Hope Encouragement and Empowerment - S.H.E.E.** that empowers women to focus on a specific faith charge each day of the week with revelatory knowledge designed to prove God's word in both power and demonstration. She is a co-author in the International Motivational Speaker, Dr. Cheryl Wood's **Women Inspiring Nations, v2** book anthology, and a co-author in Michelle Boulden-Hammond's **Silhouette of Strategies From Authentic Coaches For Mind, Body & Soul** book anthology.

Bernadette is a native Washingtonian and single mother of one daughter, Makeala. She regularly attends her church and loves volunteering. Her mission is to make a positive impact in the community, one life at a time, through influencing the personal and professional path of those she serves in her church, community, business, and she does exactly that through BB Coaching and Consulting, LLC.

Contact Information:

Email: bernadettembrawner@gmail.com

Website:https://bernadettebrawner.com

Facebook: @BBCoachingandConsultingLLC

Contact number: 202-838-7363

FAITH IN ACTION

Growing Deeper in Faith

Practical Steps to Walking in Faith

1. What does faith mean to you?

2. What does faith look like to you?

3. What fiery test have you been through and how did you handle it?

____

____

____

____

____

____

____

4. What have you read in this book that you can apply to your life?

____

____

____

____

____

____

____

5. Are you ready to share your story/testimony?

____

____

____

____

____

____

____

6. What have you learned about faith?

7. Do you allow fear to rule your life?

8. Are you ready to walk by faith?

FAITH IN ACTION

Growing Deeper in Faith

Use These Pages to Capture Your Thoughts and Write Your Story/Testimony

(Remember to put a date each time you journal)

Hebrews 11:6 But without faith *it is* impossible to please *Him,* for he who comes to God must believe that He is, and *that* He is a rewarder of those who diligently seek Him.

ISBN: 978-0-578-82434-5

www.ingramcontent.com/pod-product-compliance
Lightning Source LLC
LaVergne TN
LVHW050648100826
845148LV00011B/2038

* 9 7 8 0 5 7 8 8 2 4 3 4 5 *